Sowing In Silence

By Cheryl Settle and James Sigmon

Sowing In Silence / Cheryl Settle & James Sigmon
Photographs by James Sigmon.

Sanctuary Distribution
5265 Central Pike
Mount Juliet, Tennessee 37122
615-758-7646

Edited by Michelle Hicks

Graphic design by Stephen K. Foster & James Sigmon

Manufactured in the United States of America
First printing March 1997
Library of Congress Catalog Card Number : 97-91664
ISBN:1-57988-013-4
Product number: SS0007SB
Copyright 1997

Foreward:

There is one simple fact of life that has proven to be true throughout the ages, **you reap what you sow**. Time after time life has proven, what you give, comes back to you. Whether you sow seeds of goodness, anger, hate, or love, the saying is always true.

This book was written to give everyone ideas on sowing good things in life. The beautiful things about this is, most of these ideas can be carried out in total silence; encouraging people to simply give for the sake of giving.

As you plant these wonderful seeds in other's lives they are surly going to come back to you in an abundant harvest of blessings.

Be creative, give not to get, but for the pleasure of giving. It will enrich your life and the live of those around you.

Blessings,

Cheryl Settle and James Sigmon

Thank You from Cheryl

I'd like to dedicate this book to Floyd Hicks for teaching me to sow seeds of kindness in people's lives. When I mentioned to him my idea of encouraging others to do the same, he immediately spoke up and suggested the title, Sowing In Silence. Thank you Dad, I love you!

I'd also like to say a special thanks to James Sigmon who my husband Keith and I have grown to love with all our hearts. He is truly an example of Sowing In Silence. May God richly bless you and cause His face to shine upon you.

I thank God for all the people He has sent into my life sowing seeds of love and kindness.

Thank you Keith, Mom, Donnie, Tricia, Matthew, Mark, Melody, Billy, Michelle, Nikki, BJ, Emeigh, and all my wonderful friends.

Special thanks to Cindy Leaver and Michelle Hicks for all their long hours of hard work, typing and editing this book.

Thank You from James:

I want to dedicate this book to my mother, Nadeane Sigmon, who taught me to sow kindness, love, and compassion in life. She encouraged me to see good in people and see beauty in everyday life around us.

Thanks goes to Aimee, Stephen, and Bob without whom this project could have never been completed. You all make my life richer.

Special thanks to Keith and Cheryl Settle who are two of the best friends and business associates a person could ever have. You both hold a special place in my heart.

Thanks also to Dorthy Pile who introduced me to infrared black and white film and pushed me to experiment with many mediums of photography.

I appreciate the encouragement of my fiends, Marvin, Peggy, Jack, Aimee, Marc, Rony, Mary E., Martha, Stephen, Amy, Mandy, Sarah, Melinda, Doug, Mary, Charlie, Billy Ann, Matthew, Jonathan, Brook, Aunt Jackie, Donna D., Sharon, JoEllen, and all those people I am forgetting to mention, but who are always appreciated.

A special thank to my dad, Charles Sigmon, for always letting me follow my dreams.

Love,
James

Pick a bouquet of wild flowers and leave on a friend or neighbors front porch with a little note telling them they're special. Remember we're sowing in silence so don't sign your name. Just smile if they tell you about it.

*Call a friend when you know
she's normally not home and leave
an encouraging message on her
answering machine.*

Cut your neighbor's grass for them and don't tell them you did it.

*O*n a rainy day sit down with your child and make up a little cards with messages like "Thank You," "Have A Great Day," or a Bible verse. Leave them in a restaurant, or give to a check out clerk, or leave in a public restroom, etc. Be creative!

On holidays make cards decorated according to the seasons such as Merry Christmas, Happy New Year, or Happy Thanksgiving. It may make them take a deep breath and smile, remembering why they're celebrating in the first place.

Help someone on an airplane who has a lot of luggage find an empty bin.

When someone is rude to you, instead of reacting angrily, simply smile and say, "Hard day?"

Give a thank-you note to your mailman, garbage collector, or other service person at a time other than Christmas.

Offer a glass of water to the person
who works on your lawn
or a delivery person.

Send an anonymous note of
friendship and a compliment
to a person you don't like.
They may end up being a friend.

Record a book for a blind person or someone who is too sick to read.

When visiting someone in the hospital, stop by the gift shop and buy an inexpensive gift or flowers. Then stop by the nurses station and ask to have them delivered to someone who has no flowers.

Pray for others. This is one of the greatest ways to invest in someone's life and they never know.

Bow your head in a public restaurant and say the blessing before eating. It is a message of thankfulness to our creator. It may remind someone they are taking the simple blessings of life for granted.

Write a poem to a friend telling them what their friendship means to you. Have it framed nicely so they can display it.

If you work at a cash register for a living and someone is short of money for their purchase, offer to make up the difference.

When passing through a toll booth pay for a few cars behind you and have the toll man tell them someone has already paid for theirs. What a lift that could be for someone who is stressed out or having a hard day.

Buy a plant that has babies such as aloe or spider plants. Transplant them into little baskets filled with soil. At Easter every year, tie a yellow bow on the handle and give them as gifts. What joy you'll bring to friends, family, and co-workers.

Smile and compliment a stranger while on an elevator.

Everyone loves sourdough bread. Bake a loaf. Then give the recipe and some starter dough to a friend and tell them to keep the chain going. Just think how many people will enjoy this edible gift.

(see recipe in back)

Send cookies to work with your spouse.

Take a person to lunch that usually is the giving person. Sometimes they are taken for granted. Give back to them and you'll be blessed.

Invite an elderly couple to dinner.

If you know someone who is going through financial stress, put a note of faith with a $20, $50, or $100 bill and simply say "God will provide." Don't sign your name. It will boost their faith and remind them that if God clothes and feeds the birds and flowers, He'll take care of them.

Hug more often.
You can't love too much.

Write your boss a note of appreciation. Don't sign it. It'll mean a lot to them to know someone appreciates him without wanting anything in return.

When someone mistreats you, bake them a loaf of bread or a cake. It'll help keep you from getting caught up in grudges. You'll have a lot less stress, too!

Bake cookies for someone you'd like to get to know better and tag on a Bible verse or a poem.

(see recipe in back)

Thank your doctor or dentist for their concern or even better, send them a thank-you card.

Send flowers to someone at work that never receives any gifts. Sign the card "Just someone who thinks you're a wonderful person."

Write a note of encouragement to a public official. They're always hearing what we don't like. Let's tell them what they're doing right.

Drop a line to your pastor, Sunday school teacher, or music leader. Let them know you appreciate them and tell them something specific you like about their leadership. Tell them you're praying for them.

When you get a server who is rude or negligent, leave a great tip anyway with a note of encouragement.

Offer to baby-sit for someone who can't afford a sitter. Make up baby-sitting certificates with your phone number on them that say "Good for three hours or one night of free baby-sitting."

Have a birthday party for Jesus for the children in your neighborhood at Christmas time. Decorate a cake and have punch and play games. Don't forget to sing "Happy Birthday Jesus!"

Invite a neighbor over for a cup of coffee or tea. Enjoy talking and sharing about your families. Offer to help them if they ever need you.

Grow an indoor herb garden and give fresh herbs to your friends and family.

Here's a fun stocking pattern to make at Christmas with your child. Form an assembly line to make the stockings. Then stuff them with goodies and give them to everyone that visits for the holidays.

Take your children shopping to purchase presents for children who are in the hospital at Christmas. Make some hot chocolate and enjoy wrapping the gifts while laughing and singing Christmas music. It would be fun to carol while distributing the gifts.

Get a group of friends together for an old fashioned caroling night. Make a list of the older people you know. Go caroling at each person's house on the list. Leave them a bag of Christmas cookies.

*Cook a big Thanksgiving meal
and share it with someone who is lonely,
single, or less fortunate.*

Write a note in your child's or spouse's lunch telling them they're special and that you love them.

Get in the habit of saying "Thank you." and get in the habit of writing thank-you notes.

Laugh at a joke that no one else is laughing at.

Turn the other cheek.

Anonymously pay for piano lessons for someone that wants to take them but can't afford it.

Send the police station or fire station in your neighborhood doughnuts and a note of appreciation.

*Take your parents to lunch
for no reason.*

Forgive someone who offended you.

Unconditionally.

Seeds Of Forgiveness

© 1997 James Sigmon

Seeds Of Goodness

© 1997 James Sigmon

© 1997 James Sigmon

Seeds Of Kindness

© 1997 James Sigmon

© 1997 James Sigmon

Friends Are Forever

© 1997 James Sigmon

© 1997 James Sigmon

Someone Cares

© 1997 James Sigmon

© 1997 James Sigmon

© 1997 James Sigmon

You Make Life Nicer

© 1997 James Sigmon

Take a fun night class and pay a friends way that otherwise couldn't attend.

Befriend someone who you normally wouldn't be friends with.

Volunteer at a cancer center or
hospital for six months.

Sneak in your parent's house and surprise them by cleaning their house or shampooing the carpet.

Shovel the snow off your neighbor's sidewalk or porch.

Have a neighborhood barbecue.

*B*e a role model to a child who is neglected or orphaned.

Consider adopting an older child.

Laugh with someone who needs a good laugh.

Make a pot of homemade chicken and dumplings. Take it to friends, neighbors, or family members when they are sick.

(see recipe in back)

Write a song for someone.

Call a radio station during request time and dedicate a song to someone special in your life.

When paying bills include a bookmark with an uplifting quote, Bible verse, or poem.

Send an extra set of pictures to family or friends from a get together.

Buy a nice outfit for someone who needs a lift. Wrap it and send it special delivery. Include an invitation for a night out.

Make homemade greeting cards.

When a child comes to your door selling something for school that you really don't need, buy it anyway and let them keep it. They'll never forget you, or their lesson in giving.

At Christmas or on birthdays, give an intangible gift such as a certificate to do someone's chores for a week, cook dinner for three nights, mow the yard, or clean the bathroom. Use your imagination.

Let out of town friends stay with you while they're on vacation. You'll enjoy the change and they will. too.

Offer free baby-sitting for new parents. Offer to keep the new baby overnight to give the parents a good nights sleep.

Offer to take an older neighbor or family member to the grocery store.

Return good for evil.

Brush your cat or dog. You'd want to be brushed if you were in their shoes (paws.)

Go caroling in July. Sing old gospel hymns instead of Christmas songs. Sing at hospitals, nursing homes or cancer centers.

Give someone a second chance.

Have mercy on people you don't understand or people whose circumstances you don't relate to. Put yourself in their shoes.

Overlook an offense.

Leave a few bags of groceries on the back porch of someone having financial problems. Don't leave a note. Be sure to buy their favorite foods.

Offer to teach a teenager to drive.

Go to lunch with the person being gossiped about in the office. Extend your friendship and invite someone else, too. This might help stop the gossip.

*Love when you're tempted
to become bitter.*

Buy blankets, socks, coats, and sweaters from garage sales or thrift stores. Keep them in your car and give them to homeless people you come across.

Leave a thank-you note and a tip for the hotel maid when staying in a hotel.

Get in the habit of paying a little extra when visiting doctors, dentists, lawyers, etc. Tell them to apply it to the account of someone that may need help paying their bill.

Tell a stranger to have a good day.

*Tell a stranger or co-worker to
"Keep smiling!"*

Ask a school teacher about needy children in her class. Bring extra school supplies to be given anonymously.

Give an employee a day off with pay, just for the fun of it.

Do what is right when no one else is, encouraging others to follow. You'll be thanked one day.

Tape a quarter on a pay phone for someone who may need it.

Be kind to everyone you meet because you don't know what pain or hurt is in their life.

Pay extra on your utility bill and ask it to be given to someone whose bill is past due.

Send a bouquet of balloons to your teenager at school with a note saying, "Someone thinks you're special."

Gather items in a basket such as magazines, lotion, shampoo, lip balm or music tapes, etc and distribute them with friends to hospital patients.

Always smile at people passing by.

Cook dinner and clean the house. This will bring a smile to a spouse who has had a hard day!

When passing by a broken down car, place a call to the police for help. They'll never know you did it but you'll be glad you did.

Offer to take a disabled or elderly person to the doctor, grocery, mall, or out to lunch.

Be kind to animals. Rescue a cat or dog from the pound. They make great pets too.

Give your mom and dad a gift on your birthday.

When someone is having an unusually busy or stressful day, sow in silence by being silent..

Skee's Chicken & Dumplin's

Cook 6 chicken breasts along with 1/2 stick of butter in 8 quarts of water until tender. Remove chicken and debone. Six quarts of broth should be left.

Take 6 cups of self-rising flour
1/2 teaspoon salt
1 Tablespoon of oil
3 cups of buttermilk

Mix ingredients and roll out like a pie crust 1/2" thick. Cut into 2" x 2" squares. Add chicken back to broth and bring to a boil. Drop squares into boiling broth and cook for 40 minutes.

Cheryl's Cookies

1 cup all-purpose flour

1 1/4 cups whole wheat flour

1/3 cup wheat bran

1 teaspoon baking soda

1 teaspoon salt

2 sticks butter, softened

3/4 cup granulated sugar

3/4 cup packed light brown sugar

1 teaspoon vanilla extract

2 eggs

1 12 oounce. package semi-sweet chocolate chips

1 12 ounce package peanut butter chips

1 cup walnuts (optional)

Preheat oven to 375 degrees. Combine flour, wheat bran, baking, soda and salt. Set aside. In large mixing bowl, beat butter, sugar, brown sugar, and vanilla until creamy. Beat in eggs. Gradually add flour mixture. Add chips and nuts. Drop onto ungreased cookie sheet. Bake approximately 8-10 minutes. (Cookies look doughy when they are done.)

Sourdough Starter

(When making Sourdough Starter, never use quick-rising yeast.)

In a large bowl dissolve 1 package active dry yeast in 1/2 cup warm water. Stir in 2 cups warm water, 2 cups all-purpose flour, and 1 tablespoon sugar or honey. Stir until smooth. Cover bowl with cheesecloth and let stand at room temperature for 5 to 10 days, stirring twice daily.

To store, transfer starter to a jar. Cover with cheesecloth and refrigerate. Do not cover jar tightly with a metal lid.

To use starter, bring desired amount to room temperature. Replenish starter after each use by stirring 3/4 cup all-purpose flour, 3/4 cup water, and 1 teaspoon sugar or honey into remaining starter. Cover and let stand at room temperature at least 1 day or until it bubbles. Refrigerate for later use.

If you are not going to use starter within 10 days, stir in 1 teaspoon sugar or honey. Repeat every 10 days unless replenished.

Sourdough Bread

(The tangy flavor is the hallmark of Sourdough Bread.)

1 cup Sourdough Starter
6 cups all-purpose flour
1 package active dry yeast
1 1/2 cups water
3 tablespoons sugar
3 tablespoons butter
1/2 teaspoon baking soda   *(Preheat oven to 375 degrees.)*

Bring Sourdough Starter to room temperature. Combine 2 1/2 cups of the flour and the yeast. Heat and stir water, sugar, butter, and 1 teaspoon salt just till warm. Add to flour mixture. Add Sourdough Starter. Beat with an electric mixer on low speed for 30 seconds, scraping bowl constantly. Beat on high speed for 3 minutes.

Combine 2 1/2 cups of flour and the soda. Add to yeast mixture. Stir till combined. Using a spoon, stir in as much remaining flour as you can. (You may have a little left over.) Turn out onto a floured surface. Knead in enough remaining flour to make a moderately stiff dough. (About 6 minutes total.) Shape into a ball. Place in greased bowl; turning once. Cover; let rise in warm place till double in size (45 to 60 minutes).

Punch dough down. Turn out onto a lightly floured surface. Divide in half. Cover; let rest 10 minutes. Shape into 2 round loaves. Place on a greased baking sheet. Flatten each slightly to a 6 inch diameter or shape into 2 oblong loaves. Cover; let rise until double in size (30 minutes). Bake at 375 degree oven for 30 to 35 minutes or till done. Remove from baking sheet and cool.

All of the pictures inside this book and the cover photo were shot in black and white, printed on Agfa 118 fiber based paper, then hand-tinted using a mixture of oil paints and pencils to create these beautiful soft images.

James Sigmon